I0200775

Into the Beautiful

Poetry by Montana Artists

S. E. Thomas, M.A., Editor

Into the Beautiful

Poetry by Montana Artists
Volume I

S. E. Thomas, M.A., Editor

Published by The Dramatic Pen Press, L.L.C.

Lolo, Montana

Copyright © 2014 The Dramatic Pen Press, LLC

All rights reserved.

ISBN-10: 0692329544
ISBN-13: 978-0692329542

A great many thanks to the hardworking

English and art teachers across our beautiful state.

May your legacy of beauty continue to flourish

long after we are gone.

Table of Contents

Our Winners

Cover Art Contest Winner

Dave Noble

For the Image:

Tranquil Waters: Driftwood at Flathead Lake

About the Artist

Dave Noble is passionate about learning new things in God's amazing creation. As a kid, Dave developed an interest for weather by watching thunderstorms and tracking snowstorms in his home state of Maryland. He earned his Bachelor of Science degree in Meteorology at the University of Millersville in Pennsylvania in 1999. Dave worked in the private weather industry in Massachusetts for five years before moving to Alaska, where he endured extreme weather, including -50 F temperatures! In 2011, Dave, his wife Lisa, and their two young kids decided to warm up a bit and move to Montana, where Dave continues to work in the weather industry. On road trips with his family, he often pulls over with camera in hand to capture beauty. Life is never boring in Dave's world. Besides still photography, he likes time-lapse photography because he can see more of what occurs on the microscale meteorology level, such as the birth and dissipation of clouds. Dave also enjoys videography, skiing, cooking, building projects, reading to his kids, going on dates with his wife, singing, playing guitar, learning about nature, reading Christian biographies, picking wild huckleberries, taking road trips, shooting Nerf guns, and fishing.

Adult Poetry Contest Winners

First Place

La Luna

She calls
Wails through the night
Longing to see her love
Across the miles
Pulling at the earth to try and reach him
Only feeling his warmth in the dim hours of morning
Until she once again dips below his reach

by
Amanda Easton

About the Author

Amanda Easton was born in the West and raised in the Rockies. She is a graduate from the University of Montana's BFA program. As an artist, writing has always been another form of entering into a larger conversation. She currently calls beautiful Montana her inspiration and home.

Second Place

Wearing the Darkness

In December in Montana
The darkness fits itself down around you,
An impervious, inevitable black garment,
Heavy,
As the Earth tips away and away – from the sun.
You know winter, so you know there's no dispelling
This ubiquitous dark.
You hold out your arms and let the sleeves of it
slide onto your skin –
You believe the stars in the roof of the prairie
Will fasten themselves like sequins
To your inky cloak –
Stepping out the door,
You toss the velvety black about your neck like a scarf:
You've had a lot of practice
Wearing the darkness.

by
Holly J. Heser

About the Author

Writing poetry has been a passion for me since I was a teenager. I am a native Montanan; I grew up in the Great Falls area, and my childhood was greatly influenced by time spent on my grandparents' cattle ranch near Belt. After obtaining a degree in English from MSU-Bozeman in 1983, I taught seven years in Wolf Point. I met my husband there, and our first two children were born there. I found the vastness of prairies and badlands in eastern Montana as thrilling as the mountains to which I'd been accustomed.

In 1990, I took a teaching position in Lewistown, and our youngest child was born here. I currently teach Senior English, AP English, and Creative Writing at Fergus High School.

We now split our time between our home in Lewistown and the ranch at Belt that has been in our family for four generations. Both my husband and I feel the ranch is our true home, and we plan to retire there someday. I feel incredibly blessed to live in a state with such beauty, wildness, and magnificence.

Third Place

Winter's Final Storm

The last remaining gasps of winter lie
Upon the land.
White flakes no longer pile
In drifts, but cotton-like to earth they fly;
On soil's warmth they only last a while.
Our winter gives a last convulsive blast;
His fading hold no longer can maintain—
So feeble is his clutch, it does not last,
But slowly from his grasp we see it wane.
The grey expanse of sky, with clouds hung low,
Exhales the winter's final soggy breath;
In weary, sad resign he does let go,
With steady showers passes on to death.
What awe does winter's expiration bring;
For his decay does yield the birth of spring.

by
Allen E. Leland

About the Author

Allen E. Leland was born in Waukegan, IL to parents who were both teachers. The second of six children, Leland grew up living with his family in places such as Nevada, Montana, Kansas, and Illinois. His childhood as well as adult experiences include the big city life of Las Vegas and Chicago as well as life in the small farming communities of Judith Gap and Lustre in Montana. Leland has taught all 30 years in Big Sky Country, and currently teaches 9-12 English at his alma mater, Lustre Christian High School, which is located in the state's northeast corner. After graduating from Tabor College in Hillsboro, KS, Leland returned to Montana to stay. Leland has written an occasional poem over the years, but not much since college. In recent years, however, he has been teaching a poetry class, and his poetry students' hard work and enthusiasm for creating poetry has inspired Leland to once again create poetry of his own. Leland enjoys spending time in God's creation through camping, hunting, and fishing. He also loves spending time with family, especially his wife Connie and son Tom.

Teen Poetry Contest Winner

First Place

King Crow

Above the grassy plains, their cries of triumph ring
While down below the trees of old allow the squalling king
To wander here and wander there, he takes the rotting flesh.
His greedy beak and beady eyes attack the lifeless crest.
Feathers fall around the ground, their sheen covered red.
All the while, his majesty sits atop the royal head
Engraving a mark of pure hunger and desire
He orders the flame and controls the heat of the fire.
Protruding through this feast, the rain falls on these beasts.
Bones and wings are soon to flee but not this shallow king.
He stays and sways, his feet lose touch
For all this flesh that fills him so much.
Control is not what he knows best.
The arrogance of his blunder has stopped the clock
That ticks inside his chest.

by
Sophia Schindler

About the Author

Sophia Schindler is a senior at St. Labre High School and grew up on a ranch near Busby, Montana. She has been writing poetry, stories, and songs as a hobby and for classwork for over five years. She is class president and on the student council, but music is her primary love. She plays drums, guitar, piano, and banjo and intends to pursue the study of music composition in college, with the ultimate goal to score movie soundtracks as a career.

Sophia derives inspiration from inanimate things, like a feeling or a moment. She seeks to use very descriptive scenes. Even if she's describing a dragon's lair, the point is to get an emotion across to readers. While the subject matter is important, what it helps imprint on the reader's brain is the larger goal.

Second Place

The Valley

Needles hit the ground
Soft like rain.
A maple leaf travels downstream,
Evading rock obstacles.
A fallen log recedes into reflecting waterways.
Waves of wheat flow towards the mountains,
Washing onto their jagged base.
A rainbow of scales beam light onto river glass.
Willows sweep excess leaves into rushing water,
Nature's housekeeper.
The water moves in the form of an otter.
Movement disrupts the reflection.
Bitterroots check their shadows in the icy mirror.
Satisfied, they bend towards the trees.
The valley shudders before winter sleep.

by
Shelby Kinch

About the Author

I am 14 years old and I attend Hellgate High School. I started writing when I attended a summer writing camp at a very young age and I have continued to write ever since. I love skiing and being outdoors, so the majority of my poems focus on small details in nature or the beautiful Montana landscape. I often think of ideas for poems while skiing and hiking. I also love to write about different cultures because it challenges me to write from a different perspective and it informs the reader about that culture. I love to write ekphrastic poetry because I find art very inspiring and it requires detailed description. Many of my poems are inspired by artwork from the Missoula Art Museum. My favorite poet is Emily Dickinson because I love her writing style. Her poems have inspired me to write about nature and have shaped my writing style in many ways.

Third Place

Boring Perfection

Perfection:
No flaws,
No mistakes,
No stories.

You see,
I find perfection boring.

What great sea-faring tales were written in calm waters?
What explorers lead flawless adventures?
What stories happen in this mythical world of perfection?

In a world of chance,
Can you really keep to the plan?
We're always in a hurry,
And that just makes beauty blurry.

I find perfection boring,
As it hides beautiful stories.

by
Maddelyn Black

About the Author

My name is Maddelyn Black and, as you can read, I like to write poetry. Some other hobbies I have are reading books, reading fan fiction, taking long walks, and trying to catch up on my favorite shows. I'm inspired by practically anything that I feel any emotional connection with. This includes friends, family, pets, enemies, philosophical thinking, and heart-wrenching moments in my favorite shows. Most of my work needs extensive editing after I write it, though, as an 'inspired me' is not a fan of spelling or grammar. The main style of writing I do is free verse poetry, though I do write short stories regularly. I plan to keep writing throughout my life, as it is one of the best things that I have ever made a habit of doing. I want to grow up to be an English teacher so I can keep reading and writing well into my life.

Child Poetry Contest Winner

First Place

The Gentleman In Autumn

Giant, beautiful, red and green,
Waves at friendly people who zoom by on the street,
A giant antonym stoplight that can't make up its swirling mind,
A wonderful, kind gentleman that gives all
of his colorful garments away,
A beautiful lady that's gracefully dancing at a ball,
A grand ship that throws his passengers overboard,
A magnificent mannequin wearing the latest fashion,
I see what a tree could really be.
Do you?

by
Emmy Claire Fanguy

About the Author

Emmy is the oldest of four children. She loves to explore the outdoors, and especially enjoys climbing a large maple tree in her front yard. This tree was the inspiration for her poem because of its bright leaf color transitions each fall. Emmy was born in Starkville, Mississippi and moved to Missoula, Montana when she was four. She still enjoys visiting her family in the Deep South, where a swimming pool is the only escape from the extreme summer heat. Emmy's passions are reading mysteries, singing songs, and writing poems. In addition to her traditional 4th grade subjects in home school, Emmy really enjoys learning about animals. She has two pets of her own, a dog named Sweet Pea and a guinea pig named Samson. Emmy's parents are Joe and Kari and her siblings are Preston, Madelynn and Ethan.

Second Place

Assignment Book

a simple book
recording secrets
taking assignments
writing its own life in itself
helping its owner
staying in an empty metal locker
no longer carrying empty pages
for its own story is finished

by
Boone Smail

About the Author

I am Boone Smail, a sixth grader from Stanford, MT. I do just about anything else a twelve year old does, but maybe a bit more. Stanford is a small town in central Montana close to Lewistown. There isn't much to do here in the Judith Basin— although there are some fun things, especially when you gather friends up to play outdoors, video games, or Minecraft.

I live a week with my dad and then switch to my mom's house for a week. At my dad's I normally go to Great Falls to watch a movie and eat at a restaurant. At my mom's I either go hunting or just have fun with friends.

I used to have two dogs, but at separate times. One was an adorable six-month-old beagle I called Skylar, and the other a four-year-old boxer called Belle. I grew attached to both of them, but had to give them away because they were too much trouble.

My memories of my family, friends, and pets are what give me writing ideas.

Third Place

Misted Woods

Misted woods,
Misted mind,
Tree ahead unseen,
Thought wondering unknown,
Head brushing branches,
Ideas hinting existence,
Thorns scratching legs,
Memories reminding,
Berries juicy,
Dreams telling,
Misted forest,
Hazy mind,
Never to lift,
Never to see.

by

Ostara Serenity Alrescha

About the Author

Ostara Serenity Alrescha was born on March 20th, 2002, close to Snowflake, Arizona. She moved in 2003 to Lincoln, Illinois where her grandparents lived and where her younger brother was born in 2004. A year before she moved, Ostara attended Chesterese Elementary School for Kindergarten. In 2008, Ostara and her family moved to Missoula, Montana so her mother could transfer to Missoula's Cracker Barrel and be near the mountains her parents missed. Ostara attended Rattlesnake Elementary School for first grade. This is when she became interested in books. In 2009, Ostara and her brother began homeschooling. Interested in new things, Ostara played outdoor soccer with the YMCA. Soon afterwards, they joined the Five-Valley Homeschool Co-op for social activities. Ostara met neighborhood friends who enjoyed similar interests, and they often played at a nearby park. In 2012, Ostara joined Strikers competitive soccer and became interested in writing. Her team involvement and certain world issues inspired some of her poems and helped her in her writing. In the winter of 2012, Ostara began attending a free writing group at the local library where her writing skill grew. Ostara still lives in Missoula.

Poems by Adults

ᔆ Nature Poems ᔆ

Evening

Mountains engulf the sun like candy.
Sweet and soft breezes brush my hair while birds return to nests,
drained from early fleets and flying.
Grass waves gently,
breathing words of rippling slumber.
Tired and calm,
I close my eyes and smell the ripened plants,
not dead, only old with sharpened character.
The rose may wilt, its stem hunched down,
but awful dread it doesn't feel.
The bright new posies soon will grow their roots.
I lie upon the cool hard ground and see the early,
sneaking moon.
I sigh and smile 'cause it can't fool me.
I see the night coming, and I will not fight it.
I will embrace it in this spot.

by
Emmaline Louisa Bristow
Honorable Mention

Lightning Forest South of Darby

My dead pines, stand tall in your sickness,
an army of grey at watch against foreign eyes
in these barren hills.
Cover secret treasures of wooden wounds from peeling sheds,
Indian paintbrush kissing violet weeds,
and fresh prints from smaller hands.
Open to me in sunlight and birdsong,
in clear currents and moss whispers.
Let down your hair,
shake the burrs of winter's arrows,
and raise your arms to a newly blue heaven.
I breathe your ghosts and stolen stories,
across another season
harsh into another season giving.

by
Bridget Heather Gibbons
Honorable Mention

Beyond Yellow

Naming fall leaves "a nice yellow"
Simply doesn't do creation justice.
Why not call them gold-charged fire dancers
Or light-shocked flamethrowers?
Lying on the forest floor, they become sumptuous butter chips
Drizzled on a bed of chocolate sauce.
Glancing out my window, I see Rapunzel's tresses
Rippling and flowing with the breeze.
I glimpse upright torches, blazing sentinels,
Swaying sunshine, xanthophyll epiphany.
Slanted afternoon light injects sun's blood
Into each glowing vein and stem.
They shock, they swirl and dazzle,
Reminding me to stop and admire and applaud.
These leaves are so much more than yellow;
This creation warrants such a mighty curtsy.

by
Lisa Noble
Honorable Mention

Lost in the Hush of Paradise

LOST in the comforting stillness of Glacier time
. . . LOST
in the alluring alpine fragrance
in the saturated dollops of color blanketing the mountainside
in the gentle pirouette of falling leaves
in the majesty of snowcapped pinnacles
in the faint whisper of the cascading falls
in the obstinate warming rays of the setting sun
in the instant cool of the meadow's long shadow
in the quiet company of each other and thoughts of loved ones
LOST . . .
in the hush of God's Paradise . . . .

by
Christine Maillet
Honorable Mention

Lilac

It's no wonder
The centuries are layered in mystery;
the passage of time an enigma
When each day
Enfolds its own eternity:
Consider
The lilac blossom in May –
How it constitutes its own purple universe –
Blooming in an unguarded instant.
We pass by its fruition,
We move on
To what we must do,
While its petals of petite flower-flesh
Wait for us to notice,
To enter
Their delicious life -- their palpitant world of lavender and sun.

by
Holly J. Heser
Honorable Mention

God

The mountains strained toward the sky,
So proud and tall.
But I did not notice as I passed by.
I did not look at all.
The sun blazed forth in glory bright,
Flashing colors as it raced toward night....
The trees whispered and sighed
As the wind slipped through,
And called to me, but I denied
The call. I had too much to do.
A tiny voice did still my flight:
My grandson, in the evening light.
He uttered just one childish "Oh!" filled with awe,
Wonder-washed and spellbound.
I looked about and finally saw…God.

by
Patricia Stewart-DeTonancour
Honorable Mention

Hey, Billy Goat
Hey, Billy Goat,
Where ya goin'?
Whatcha doin'?
Who ya seein'?

Do ya have a Lady Goat
Hopin' you'll walk her way today?
Do ya have some Billy Goat Buddies
Loiterin' at the local grass patch?
Do ya have a Mama Goat
Hollerin' a mean "baa" to get home early?

Hey, Billy Goat,
Where ya goin'?
Whatcha doin'?
Who ya seein'?

And why are ya so much like me?

by
Meg Elizabeth Smith

From "Conversations with a Squirrel"
He is obsessed with nuts.
Despite my most fierce attempts,
His soliloquy on the many types of nuts
Continues.
His small furry tail twitches with each passing stanza
Marking off the meter like a metronome.
He gesticulates wildly, drawing me closer,
Enticing me,
To his little, hyper body,
Vibrating with the enthusiasm of his speech.
Abruptly,
It's over.
He stole my peanuts.

by
Meg ElizabethSmith

Beautiful Montana

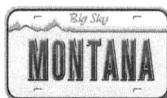

Beautiful sunrise,
Beautiful sky,
Beautiful mountains,
This new home of mine.
Beautiful water,
Beautiful night,
Beautiful sunset,
This new home of mine.
Beautiful people,
Beautiful lives,
Beautiful prairie,
This new home of mine.
Beautiful harvest,
Beautiful snow caps,
Beautiful Montana.

by
Karen Johnston

Sunset

Sunset Golden, orange
Shimmering, glowing, changing
Breathtaking beauty unlike anywhere else
Dusk

by
Michael Moll

Trees

Jazzy branches
stick in every direction
dancing to the breeze
whistling through leaves
each sing an original tune
each jive a unique way

by
Emmaline Louisa Bristow

Morning

My heart beats slowly,
the breeze is sweet with dew and soil.
The morning mist has barely set atop the drowsy flowers.
Buds of blue wake slowly, too,
before the sun has let its rays bloom out
and coat the ground with sparkling light.
The clouds stain pink with purplish glow
as birds sing gently away the night;
they mark the spring with songs of love
that fleet and flow into the sky.
Shadows start tall and long while cool silhouettes of dark
branches contrast the blue morn's haze.
Horizon lights along mountain rims awake the day.
Stretching, dawn is broken and beams stream forth,
piercing the lying world.
With that great crack the night then dies.

by
Emmaline Louisa Bristow

Trickles of the Soul

Mighty river moves below.
Moving towards one simple goal.
Many paths for inventive roaming.
Seasonal boundaries constant molding.
Ancient bed... keeps it whole.
Moving forward with boldness flowing.
Swirls, waves, something's raging.
Quietness in a simple hole.
Happy side channel to and fro.
Glistening jaunt... forever changing.
Musical poetry from the soul.
Calling attention to which way it goes.
Edges in width force dramatic creating.
Choices made with the smallest of knowing.
Powerhouse simply... continues to roll.

by
Susan Boelman

Late Spring
It's April in Montana,
as 50 mph winds blow.
Yesterday I saw some flowers,
today they're under snow.

Last week the sun came out,
and I got out my sunglasses.
But I saw the snow clouds comin',
and signed up for knitting classes.

One day I started a garden,
but by 9:00 it was too late.
I saw the squall a'comin',
and ran inside the gate!

For a minute the sun came out,
and I saw my truck was dirty.
Then the snow began to fall,
and so now it looks real pretty.

by
Brenda Hughes

❧ Poems About Relationships ❧

Couple Steps

Welcome to the matrimony dance.
It's like that, being a team—
One twirls while the other supports,
And both must learn to move to the same music.
For the dancers to glide as if they were one body,
For true fluid motion to occur
And something beautiful to take place,
Both partners have to be willing to bend
In ways they never have before.
Each individual sacrifices sprained ankles and missteps
While becoming more flexible than dreamed possible.
Each dancer learns willingness to compromise
Choreography preferences
To grow in a style that is uniquely personal
Yet colored by the style of their partner,
Their fellow manipulator of gravity and sinew,
Time and possibility.
May this dance continue to shape us into one movement,
And may it last as long as we have breath.

by
Lisa Noble
Honorable Mention

Mother

You gave us unconditional love from the time we were so small.
You did your very best tirelessly giving us your all.
There is a magical bond between a daughter and mother;
it is so perfectly special and creates a love like no other.
Now that we are all grown, this will be forever true
we promise you.
Dearest mother, we will always love you.

by
Melissa A. Skaggs

Sunshine of My Life

Before Valentine's Day,
I knew of only one sun.
Since that February day,
my life has just begun.
Within seconds,
I heard your cry….
Amid tears,
I praised God as I looked to the sky.
With showers of chocolates,
flowers and fun,
Beyond all my dreams,
Nathan,
Is the love for you… my son.

by
Christopher Heiland

Sunshine of My Life - Part II

My son is sunshine.
He brightens my every day.
His laugh is radiant and warming.
He's the biggest star in my planet.
Shine Ultra magnanimous Nathan, shine!

by
Christopher Heiland

Sunshine of My Life, Part III

There once was a boy named Nat,
Who shagged down "pop flies" with his hat.
He loved playing baseball,
During Spring,
Summer and Fall.
And Winter… well,
that was the name of his bat.

by
Christopher Heiland

To Hope With Love
I feel myself falling, no means of prevention
Wiping away every single intention
I don't want to love you, but somehow I must
Accept your imperfections and learn to adjust
We may not always receive what we want
But we will always become who we want
When feeling down, hopeless and full of despair
Remember all one really wants in this life is to be
Without a care
Hope is defined as those who never gave up and
Used what little energy they have left to rebuild
And keep moving forward.
Keep in consciousness once hopes and joys die, your
Innocence weaken of both heart and mind
Yourself should be your deepest fear and your
Worthy opponent.
It is a burden off one's soul to know their deepest
Fear is something they have already conquered
To hope with strength you weren't aware of

by
Jessica Elizabeth Kirn

For Mother's Day
We went to sea, just you and me
By train into the ship.
And when the sun came up again,
She birthed us on the sand
For thence we travelled far and wide
In many a foreign land.
By car, by bus, by train, on foot, by horse,
Alas... by cane!
We went to see, just you and me,
How other folks might live,
And then came home, for home is best,
Beneath the great pine trees.

by
Adina McCloy

❧ Poems About Heritage & Legacy ❧

Mountain Child
I am birthed with pebbles
under my feet
and granite in my veins.
I breathe the throaty pines
and whisper mists
to flames in autumn rains.
And blessed am I, my roots
entwined in land
that gives and curses life—
I thirst for glacial snows,
and that royal
abundance given anew,
and will hawk's feathers take
stone bones to flight
that you may be blessed, too.

by
Theresa Kirkpatrick
Honorable Mention

A Lifetime of Purpose
A lifetime of purpose does not appear magically
On some distant horizon as an oasis.
It sneaks up behind you and taps you on the shoulder
After years of tiny steps and a nose
Permanently halved by the grindstone.
Illusions dance their hypnotizing jig and call out catchy tunes
To distract your feet,
But a path is made by walking,
A future grown by a step, then a step, then a step.
Sometimes it seems almost mechanical, this stepping,
Like a parking meter coldly clicking off the hours.
Sometimes the steps seem erratic, haphazard,
Like a random number that ends up ringing Tokyo.
But were it not for the steps, the marrow of life would be ashen,
The gravestone dash meaningless.

And we know, the sun rises every morning
Oh, that each step would be a sunrise on the way to glory!

by
Lisa Noble
Honorable Mention

Sometime in Early February
Much in the same fashion that keepsakes are held dear,
unable to be thrown from the family china closet, or mantle,
or attic the shed stands in a North by Northeastern Montana gale
braced against the wintry weather,
gathering sagebrush and the last,
meandering piles of nomad snow
congregating by its lower, rotted boards.
My father will not put it to rest even though
there is no longer paint, no longer stain,
and it no longer holds shovels, hens, buckets of nails,
or any hope
that some pioneer will come to replace the trusses,
replace the shingles once blown across the prairie
towards the Great Missouri.
For spite, he says but not of what,
like the young ash that grows and holds the southern wall in
malevolence of the elements.
The shed houses a family of mice.
So it stands, crooked and mighty.

by
Adam Restad
Honorable Mention

❧ Poems About Women ❧

A Woman of Parts
Long beauty curves,
appealing high noon suns wear the hands of atom,
caressing waves raggedly.
Spot my eyes,
translucent daze.
Temporary,
my pupils,
universe of breaking crust,
salivating mouths gracefully.
Torn,
weary clotheslines.
Stinging rain,
forsaken wine,
drops of womanly flavor,
clasping palmed fragility.

by
Christopher Devon Loewen

Madonnas
If I could run and teach the world one thing
I'd walk into a parlor brave and tall,
and to the women
I would proudly sing of changes made
that they don't need at all.
I'd kiss the polish from their weary hands,
breathe in the poison from their greying curls,
unlock them from the prison chains of brands,
and blow away their tattoo ink in swirls.
I'd laugh the lipstick from their smiles bright,
give each a nimbus to replace their heels,
break pocket mirrors that haunt their thoughts at night,
and show them how acceptance truly feels.
But all these I can only dream and say in hopes
they'll learn and teach themselves one day.

by
Bridget Heather Gibbons
Honorable Mention

The Vogue

Like temple girls in Eastern lands, they dance.
Gyrating hips, flexing breasts, painted eyes
Stare blankly at the screen
Hungry eyes of men, stare back at them.

Like temple girls, the gods they serve
Make motions on the wall,
Exploded faces scream in monotone,
From black voices scream their agony.

Drums, like those that call the demons,
Subdue the human heart.
All is lost… null… void
Hypnotized, mesmerized; the devils sing.

Every night they come
Like temple girls in Eastern lands
To give their souls away.

by
Adina McCloy
Honorable Mention

❧ Spiritual Poems ❧

David

Stolen away.
The deceiver took his hope
And then he tempted him
To throw away the breath of life—

Hands with nails like knives
Those nails which pierced
My Savior's hands, his feet, his side
Like a cobra, wrapped around his life—

And then as final death set in
Those nails tore into us
And raped our hearts—
He stole our David away.

by
Adina McCloy

❧ Miscellaneous Poems ❧

A Ticking Clock
Lying on a blanket of luscious green,
I look up to the sky and see a pillar of red,
flaunting its emerald crown.
The bricks encase a sphere of time,
ticking silently away as forgotten moments slip by.
Grey sky mourns the seconds that will never return,
an unyielding shield against blinding light.
Its teardrops threaten to taint our emotionless day.
Columns of wood stand erect,
arms reaching out to comfort the sky in a loving embrace.
Witnessing it all are the students,
bustling about with an eagerness to fill their empty heads.
Lack of sleep plays on their faces,
as they regret the months of late night study sessions,
and frat parties.
Too tired to notice that the world continues to revolve
without them.

by
Madison Rose Hinrichs

Words on a Page
Words on a page show beauty,
Words on a page show rage.
Words on a page give us hope,
Words on a page give us courage.
Words in a lullaby; words on the stage,
All start out as words on a page.
Words bring us comfort,
Words bring us pain,
Words that start out as words on a page.

by
Karen Johnston

Questions
Why, oh wonder!
What happened to why?
Sheer, veneer!
Abysmal hued sky.
Hope's fretting ceased,
I don't have to lie.
Apollo's echo feared
Opals of a tortoise-cat's eye.
Bright freckles, be-speckled,
All over, I sigh.
Again and again I choke back my cry.
For all this,
is the answer!
So why do we,
ask why?

by
Christopher Devon Loewen

Impossible Dream
Is it possible to bless the world today?
With so much anger, destruction,
and mass amounts of hate,
diseases that kill endlessly day by day.
Where is the love? Is it hiding in the land, sky, or sea
Or in my chest
Hibernating in a deep, deep sleep
To have a blessed world today
We need to have a truce for peace.
But humans come with opinions.
And different opinions make peace
The impossible dream.

by
Tristen Alexander Guillot

Warmth of Connection

Pressing strings to match the sand and rust that,
cleverly enough you had let burn.
Dragged and pulled off ash filterless in your identity,
for once.
Beauty will find
Our letters and angles.
They're dry near the furnace,
that depth heats the soul.

by
Christopher Devon Loewen

Poems by Teens

❧ Nature Poems ❧

Montana Autumn

Grass gets brittle and golden.
Leaves tell tales...
from green to yellow to orange.
Nipping Autumn Air...
whispering through valleys.
Hardy Apple Trees gleaming with beautiful crimson fruit.
Everybody busily harvesting.
Everything bustling to beat the snow...
prepared or not.
Sheets of white cascade...
Giving thanks to a past summer.
Spring rolls around...
Shining hope for a new beautiful summer.

by
Baylee Lawrence
Honorable Mention

Bat Sounds

Chip chip chee
You may come looking for me
Chip chip choo
I'll never make an appearance for to you
Squeak squeak
I'll sometimes take a peak
Squack squack
I'll never come back
Click click
Make a wise pick
Chirp chirp
Some think I slurp
Scree scree
I'll fly free
Scrae Scrae
These are prices I'm not willing to pay

by
Taylor Elena Mee

Wave
I'm full of innocence and life.
On days of grey I'm fierce and full of danger.
Despite my mild appearance
I have the power to destroy everything lying in my path at the
time of a disaster.
My temperature rapidly changes from day to season.
I'm an unpredictable wave.

by
Baylee Lawrence

Gold
I am Everywhere.
Yet few possess me
I'm considered rare
And everyone knows me.
I hide in the seams,
of the rich and greedy.
I live in the dreams,
Of the poor and needy.
I am
Everywhere.

by
Seth J. Dustin

Musings
Grass is green,
Bear is black.
Can I have my candy back?

by
Dylan Miller

Thoughts from the Obscurity
Nobody, nowhere, no one knows the night like I do.
Black, beautiful, broken
a sky shining and hiding.

See, don't you?
See the stars...
And all the parts that are in between.
Like the bitterness of people born;
the brightness of dreams.
The night.
Hiding, haunting, holding you captive with her endless entirety.
Watch as the words you think in your deepest, most desolate
contemplations
fly fast to her.
The night.
Who nobody, nowhere, no one knows like I.

by
Dusty Sue Keim

Falls Peak
Wake up to the weeping waterfall of the rippling hills
look to the steppe that leads to the lonesome peak
Breathe in the air as it rushes away
As your soul swims to its peak
To see that the world you left wasn't so bleak

by
Philip Vial

❧ Poems About Relationships ❧

Time

we smile a last smile and this is it.
the end of an era; the end of our time.
we smile a first smile.
nervous eye contact and this is it...
the beginning of an era; the beginning of our time.
people come and people go
like birds in flight
like stars in the night.
hiding, presenting, leaving, staying.
people holding pieces of each other
this sacred, beautiful confusion.

by
Dusty Sue Keim
Honorable Mention

The Mother I Love

Mother I love your wisdom, your courage, and your strength,
to always show your feelings even if it's pain.
Mother I love your warmth and the way you love me.
You were always there to put the Band-Aid on my knee.
Mother I love your hugs, how you hold me long and tight.
It's little things like these that help me sleep at night.
Mother I love your love and all your love for me.
It's because of this that you have helped me see:
That mother I love myself; it's all because of you.
I did not know who I was, but now I know who.
Mother I love myself because of all that I've been through,
that now I find happiness in everything I do.
Mother I love myself and this is something new,
but now I see the beauty you see in front of you.
You showed me what love is.
Sometimes you don't need two.

by
Sarah Anne Milton

❧ Poems About Experience ❧

Freshman December

The snow bites cold at my cheeks
I drench my head in its powder
I've not been home now for weeks
and I exhale my breath in plumes
Few faces walk around me
with haste to get warm inside
The cold is foreign to them, but I feel homeland ties
My jeans at the knees are soaked through,
so I stand and squint my eyes
For the sun is shining hard today, demanding all abandon sight
My fingers are stiff and white,
but there's a tree I've eyed for a while
I cross the quad to embrace it, and feel the earth for miles
Some of my peers pass with stares, heading for the student café
I tag along for hot chocolate, and say goodbye to heartache.

by
Sophia Schindler
Honorable Mention

Take a Second

You are awakened,
Whether it be by the glowing morning sun,
shining through your window,
Or your screeching alarm clock,
Or maybe even by the bouncing of children
in your ever shrinking bed.
Thoughts of breakfast fill your mind as you walk to the kitchen,
That no matter how many times you say, "There is no food."
There will always be food.
Then rushing out the door you go.
It doesn't matter if you have two things planned for the day
or twenty,
Time always seems to fly,
Much faster than you realize.
But take a second and
Look around.

Enjoy the little blessings that you may miss running around.

by
Macy Shea
Honorable Mention

The Smell of Montana
The crispy burning marshmallows are very hot and gooey.
The marshmallows melt as soon as you put it in your mouth.
It sticks to the roof of your mouth like sticky peanut butter.
You have to roll your tongue on the top of your mouth
till it eventually comes off.
Burn it, peel it off.
Burn it, peel it off.
Repeat this 'till eventually it is gone.
All of a sudden it's gone, all gone.
Then my sister hands me a new marshmallow.
We roast it together in the campfire,
As we watch the stars in our favorite camping place
In Montana.

by
Madelynn Shulund

The Evil Has Landed
The sky began to fall ripping
opening a path up to heaven
time slowed to a crawl
Early morning September eleventh
steel crumbling frames
the scales of justice are decimated
hate ignites the flames
New York City incinerated
see the flames on the river
could this be judgment day
time to stand and deliver
when evil flies our way . . .our way
Tower got hit with a steel bird with wings of destruction
as the buildings split the skyline has been deconstructed

innocent blood spilled
Extremists plotting a holy war
see the flames on the river
Terrorism sealed our fate
praying hands of a killer reciting a sermon of hate
Will you please reconsider if this is to deliver
when evil flies our way. . .
flies our way
We will pick up the pieces
we never cast the first stone
through all the bereavement
we will rebuild our home

by
Terry Cody Swims Under

❧ Poems About Emotion ❧

Follow the Dreams of Your Heart
Follow the dreams of your heart.
Beat to the rhythm of your soul.
Let the music play,
While the worries of the day…
f a d e a w a y.

by
Ali Warren

Sticks and Stones
When life gives you lemons, make lemonade.
Sayings like that are just a charade.
They make things and break things with a pottery wheel,
But in the end, there's no real deal.
They come up with words that are so overplayed.
They tell you you're wrong whenever you've strayed.
You walk a fine line, and stand holding your breath,
Waiting for oral delivery of death.
So sticks and stones will break my bones,
And I will attempt to cover my groans.
But if we end the verbal havoc we wreak,
Then we can return to the light from the bleak.

by
Julia Kay Tonne

❧ Spiritual Poems ❧

Nature of God

The leaves will fall, just like us all,
If we don't follow Jesus.
There is no way He can free us.
There is a change in the colors….
God is above all others.
It's starting to get cold….
God never gets old.
The grass is dormant….
God is informant.
The sun sets behind the mountain….
God's love is flowing like a fountain.
The sun is the light for the day.
The Son is the light for our way.
Just like the rain brings life to earth,
The Holy Spirit brings life through rebirth.

by
Ashley McGee

Reflections of God

I think the moon reflects God;
How bright He is,
How He's not a fraud,
How this world is His.
The trees reflect God;
How He helps us grow,
How sometimes we get sawn,
How he makes snow.
The sun reflects God;
How He has a burning bravery,
How He is very broad,
How He is always savoring.

by
Kama Muccie

Miracle Maker

I love You so, even when I'm feeling low.
You turned the bad into good,
Even when I didn't think You could.
You heal the sick and make the blind to see,
Even when the doctors say it cannot be.
Sometimes You make the dead alive when You arrive.
Lord, You are a blessing!
That is me, confessing.
You make me smile,
And it is worth my while.
You are not a faker, Lord.
You are a miracle maker.

by
Ali Warren

❧ Miscellaneous Poems ❧

Black

Dark shadows casting inside n' out...
My shade is permanent.
I'm so dark, I'm invisible...
Darkening the slightest of slight brilliance.
Full of boldness, evil and sorrow.
Never to be associated with good...
Beautiful in my own special ways.
I oppose bright white,
Only to be sought in the midnight shadows....

by
Baylee Lawrence

Alien

I don't know where I am
But there's a man with sticky hands.
And the planet out that window is not Earth but rather purple.
The Lounge is serving stardust and I think I'm eating blue rust.
Is this another galaxy?
Or just a Star Wars fantasy?
We'll I don't know where I am,
and I don't really have a plan,
so I'll just stay with this man and his very sticky hands.

by
Sophia Schindler

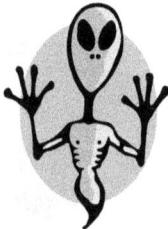

Poems by Children

❧ Nature Poems ❧

The Ocean
the cool salty air I breathe
the love and beauty is back in my heart
sand beneath me is my pillow
part of my life
warm water rushing up to me as if we are friends
the sound is like the comfort
of a soft feather
the sparkling water
afar a journey
waiting for its companion to follow
I have awakened to my unknown love
I had lost the pillow beneath me
my friend
the first touch of water
I know I am home where I belong

by
Ellie Kay McCluey
Honorable Mention

Dolphins
The sun is setting in the west,
Glorious colors everywhere.
But as I lay my head to rest,
I hear a distant quiet splash.
A beautiful dolphin twirling there,
Dancing through the sea.
And as I see the dolphin fair,
I find ten thousand more.
Leaping and calling in the ocean,
They swim away from me.
With a sleek and graceful motion,

They disappear from sight.
Gliding into the arriving night.

by
Autumn Conway
Honorable Mention

The Sea

I stand o'er the water—that sea of sapphire blue,
And as I watch the seagulls fly,
I wonder where they go to.
And those things that we call fishes, do they explore the sea?
Or do they remain in the reef, hiding from dangers they see.
What about the little crabs, scurrying out of sight?
Do they prefer the dark, or do they like daylight?
All these creatures live by the sea, surviving off of it,
Some by stealth, some by wit,
But they depend upon the sea.
They all depend upon the sea.

by
Autumn Conway

A Bird

I fly over the ocean.
I fly over the sea.
I fly over the ocean.
You will see me in the spring.

by
Emily Ziegler

The Elephant

The elephant is gray.
They eat hay.
You might have seen one at the bay.
They go there a lot.
The elephant has big, floppy ears,
With wrinkles all over.
The elephant has two small eyes;
They might have tears.
Drip, drop… Drip, drop… Shooo, shooo…
The elephant sounds like a waterfall.
They work as a group.
Have you ever seen one play ball?

by
Katelyn Warren

The Adventures of Gale

Gale jumped on a whale.
It started to hail.
He grabbed a pail,
but slipped on a snail.
He fell down a trail,
While trying to bail
Some ginger ale,
And met his new best friend, Dale.
He went to school,
Jumped in the pool,
And thought he was cool.
He fell off a boat,
Onto a goat,
And started to float.

by
Braydn Muccie

Wonders
Sometimes I wonder of a time that never ends
that pretenders always believe in.
Snowflakes fall and cover the Earth
never telling why they fall
and why they always make the Earth so cold.

by
Hope Jasmin

Trees
trees towering tall
colossally above all
stretching mightily

by
Boone Smail

Beautiful Forest
trees on the peak of the mountain
swaying with the wind
green blanket over the alps
creating life for the forest

by
Zack Solomon

Nature in the Sky
nature so beautiful
attraction in the sky
sky so colorful
colorful as art
starts like a maze
a maze in defiance

by
Isaac Claver

Wilson

Wilson is fuzzy and fun
and he loves to run.
He eats apples and oats
and is friends with goats.
He plays with foals
and rolls and rolls.
He is my favorite equine
and he is divine.

by
Danya Khonke

Mountains

Blue and green from a distance.
Elegant.
Amazing.
Naturally graceful, rugged, and appealing.
Like a picture from God.
At night like silhouettes, mysterious yet warm.

by
Caleb Currier

Grasshopper

Grasshopper
Golden,
Fast playing, chirping, hopping
Noisy hopper
Bug

by
Indio Moll

The World

The world—colors so bright
Full of all your wondrous light
All the animals alive and free
Running around happy as can be
All the trees and all the life
They have yet to start to strive

So much green and all the colors
This all brings me many wonders
All the animals wild and tame
They will never be the same
Wild animals won't obey
They go around and chase their prey

by
Sierra Jo Reese

**The following is a collection of acrostic poems produced by
some of the kindergartners and 1st Graders from Pablo
Elementary School.**

Mountain lion
flOwer
suNset
buTterfly
Ants
raiNbow
bAsketball

by
Alice Wolf-Black
Kindergarten

Mountain
gOat
suNset
Tree
Ants
raiNbow
bAsketball

by
Tory Pierce
Kindergarten

Mountains
Owl
Nice
Tree
bAts
gNats
Antelope

by
Shawnte' Erickson
1st Grade

Mountain lion
Osprey
Nature
Tower
Ants
gNats
grAass

by
Wilcoxson Martinez
1st Grade

Mountains
rOcks
robinN
Trees
blAck bear
suNshine
Antelope

by
Jerrime Smith-White
1st Grade

The following is a collection of cinquain poems produced by the 3rd and 4th graders from Pablo Elementary School.

Bobcats
Short tails, pointy ears
Climbing, hunting, jumping rock to rock
They live in the mountains
Cats

by
Molly Spotted Eagle
4nd Grade

Chickens
Feathers, wings
Running, pooping, wondering,
They are fast
Birds

by
Brent Lozeau
3rd Grade

Bison
Big, brown
Eating, plowing, living
It is speedy
Buffalo

by
Shelby Carpentier
4th Grade

Horses
Beautiful, black
Jumping, galloping, running,
They are strong
Animal

by
Anna Marie Paul
4th Grade

Brown Bears
Mean, fast
Eating, hunting, drinking,
They are protective
Amazing

by
Aliya DeRoche
4th Grade

Trees
Tall, round
Growing, moving, falling,
Make fire wood
Heavy pine trees

by
Randy Blixt
3rd Grade

Grizzly Bear
Hump on its back
Eating, fishing, sleeping
It eats prey
Bear

by
Owen Blixt
3rd Grade

Horse
Tall, white
Eating, playing, running
Calm, playful
Animal

by
Maizy Blixt
4th Grade

Wild Life
Lively, beautiful
Chasing, jumping, clawing
Open space living
Wild animals

by
Nikki Kendall & Rylie Wurster
3rd Grade

Fox
Fast, sneaky
Eating, hunting, drinking
They are sly
Kit

by
Gary Myers
4th Grade

Buffalo
Hairy, old
Helping, eating, running
Protects others
Bison

by
Mikenzie Morigeau
4th Grade

Black Bears
Black, big
Eating, attacking, clawing
Attacks you
Bears

by
Payton Mays
3rd Grade

❧ Poems About Montana ❧

The Place for Everyone
The best place in the whole United States,
It's by far the greatest of the greats
Its views and mountains go on for far,
And at night, for everyone, there is a star
Its activities last forever and ever,
There isn't one moment where it's not exciting—never.
The snow-capped mountains, the beautiful flowers,
Goodness! I could go on for hours!
The waterfalls and fishing spots,
Me oh my, there's lots and lots.
There's frogs to catch and bears to see;
Montana's amazing, don't you agree?
With all these sights and tons of fun,
I'm thinking: this is the place for everyone.

by
Taylor Dare Gray
Honorable Mention

Simple Gift
i am in a little town
unneeded and small
yet to me it's the best of them all
say what you may
and say what you might
but i feel right here
through day and through night
i don't wish to go
to any place else
because the chance given to live here
to me is an obviously mere simple gift

by
Boone Smail

O God, Bless the World, Big World
I will write to bless the world
For the world is crazy and grim
But there is a place in
That is sweet and good
For death can tell
This place is called Montana
Montana has its own way of life
Montanans love and don't hate
for they have all they need
they have sweet berries
they have water they can swim in
without fish floating in it or wheels coming to float
the world is blessed for they have Montana
the world always has a war to fight
the world will die if places don't become like Montana

by
Nikolay Shved

Montana
Breathtaking Montana
Powerful waters
Enormous Rocky Mountains
Historical plains

by
Sydney Von Bergen

The following is a collection of 3/5/3 poems produced by the 1st and 2nd graders from Pablo Elementary School on the theme: "Beautiful Montana."

I love Montana
Grizzlies, snakes, flowers
Bears and squirrels

by
Bailee Woll
1st Grade

The berries, yummy
The smell is fresh outside
Rain is water

by
A'Dein Hewankorn
1st Grade

Still, freedom, bears
Run fast, bobsled,
Bug, play, tree

by
Brodee Woll
1st Grade

Mountains
Are bright on top
Of the mountain

by
Saraea Wells
2nd Grade

Snakes, water, bears,
A snake swims in the water
Grass, bugs, fish

by
Chad Higgins
2nd Grade

Tree bugs run
Rain, green, reds, can play
Bears are yellow

by
Lovelei Charlo
2nd Grade

Tree, leaves, freedom,
Great big grizzly bear plays
Horses run and play

by
Clara DeRoche
2nd Grade

Big, huge mountains
Green, red, yellow
Colors everywhere

by
Amaiya Black
2nd Grade

I love Montana
Happy people swim in golden
rivers
Freedom

by
Talayna Endfield
2nd Grade

I love Montana
Swimming at the lake,
refreshing
Grasshopper hop slow

by
NeTaous Hewankorn
2nd Grade

Trees, bugs skip
Fresh green air, feels like freedom
Games, still, bears

by
Terrance Blixt
1st Grade

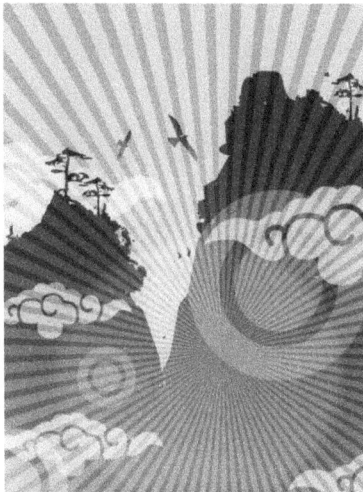

❧ Poems About Emotion & Experience ❧

Hope
Hope is a bird
With powerful wings
Caring for others
Gripping onto the edges of souls
Captivating people with magic
Relieving their matters
Getting rid of all your fears

by
Sydney Von Bergen
Honorable Mention

✎ Spiritual Poems ❧

God's Glory in the Seasons

On top of the mountain, there is a lot of activity.
With flowers blooming and new life everywhere,
spring is in the air.
It reminds me of being born again and of God's care.
In the summer heat, my thoughts of God can't be beat,
Where green shows that everything is growing
Just like I am growing in my faith in Jesus to share.
In autumn, when leaves fall from the trees up so high,
I look past them to see God's glorious sky.
Blue is what I see, which reminds me of Jesus's love,
deep as the sea.
With snow falling in the winter and covering the mountains,
White is everywhere, Just like Jesus makes me white as snow.
If I look at the mountains through the year,
I feel God's glory is always near.

by
Thomas Blomquist

Thank you, God

Thank you, God, for creating me.
Your glory is all I need.
Thy love for me is bigger than a tree.
I'm your child indeed.
God, you are great;
God you are grand;
You are never late.
Thank you for being my helping hand.
You set me free from the chains

That once held me with guilt and pain.
You are Alpha and Omega,
Beginning and End.
You forgive and forget.
You're my savior and friend.

by
Katelyn Warren

❧ Miscellaneous Poems ❧

Winter Camo
winter camo is plain awesome
winter camo is a cool mixture of colors
winter camo is a coyote running free
winter camo tastes like water
smells like earth after it rains
sounds like hunting
winter camo feels wild
winter camo looks like brush in the snow
winter camo makes me want to hunt with Dad

by
Ace Becker

Through My Eyes
I wrote this poem to bless the world,
I am not writing this poem to win a prize,
I just want people to see through my eyes,
I think that people are beautiful creatures,
they possess so many amazing features,
you cannot rule the world by possessing hate,
you need to do something good to change your fate,
I hope this poem inspires you,
to do something good for yourself and the people around you.

by
KayLynn M. Wolf

Green

green is a really big houseplant
green is a fun ball that I play with a lot
green is a smelly dead mouse
green is a sweet piece of gum
green tastes like grapes
green smells like grass
green sounds like a wolf
green makes me feel happy
green is the funnest color

by
Paul Blank

Music

I really love to sing;
Country, rock, and guys with bling;
All forms of music are found in Montana
From all types of people who wear a bandana.

Music is a form of healing,
It can change the way you're feeling.
To some it is a gift or present;
It can usually make you feel more pleasant;

Music can come from anywhere,
It gives mankind something to share.
It makes a bond 'tween you and me,
Even though we're parted by the sea.

Listening to music can be fun,
Music blesses everyone.

by
Jessica Downard

Publisher's Prerogative

First Discoveries

A naked child
Played and cooed;
His age was
Two or three.
He ran along
The sandy shore
Like sunshine
On the breeze.

He spotted
Something
Burrow deep;
And curious
As he was,
He squatted
Like an Indian chief
And watched
A sand flea buzz.

Soon his interest
Lost its wax,
And a shell
Did take its place.
He picked it up
With chubby hands
And brought it
Near his face.

The sound of waves
Did catch
His ear
And amazed
Was he to find,
That trapped
Inside such small
A land
Was a sea
Of different kind.

By S. E. Thomas
Publisher

Special Thanks!

The Starving Artist Café & Art Gallery

Come enjoy a wide variety of art while sipping great coffee & smoothies or feasting on downtown's best bakery goods. Being that we are an art centered café, we focus on featuring "starving" artists whose work would normally go unnoticed by the general public. This can range from paintings, photos, sculptures, music, jewelry or even poetry. Our artists range from professionals to young artists just starting in local grade schools. Come "Please Your Palette!" on multiple levels with art, customer relationships, and excellent food or drinks!

www.missoulastarvingartist.com

About Our Contest

The book cover and the poems in this book were collected through a state-wide poetry contest entitled, "Into the Beautiful Poetry Contest." This is an annual contest open to artists of all ages. It begins in August or September and runs through October 15th. If you are interested in entering this contest or sharing this information with a friend or family member, please bookmark the following informational resources:

Website: www.thedramaticpen.com

Facebook: www.facebook.com/thedramaticpen

Twitter: @TDPPress

You can also sign up for our free, monthly e-newsletter through the contact page on our website. All upcoming contests, calls for writers, and new products are announced there, as well as tips for writers, a book of the month, and a tried and true recipe!

More From:

@TDPPress
www.thedramaticpen.com
facebook.com/thedramaticpen

Longing for Rest
A Novella
By S. E. Thomas

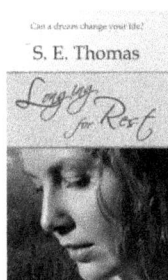

One heartbroken woman battles insomnia. Another cannot escape the coma trapping her between dreams and reality. Though they have never met, through a miraculous crossing of consciousness, they find themselves together on a grassy hill surrounded by a mysterious fog. In this dream world, Amy and Gracie form an unusual friendship. But, will fear, pain, and betrayal follow them and spoil this haven? Will they finally be able to rest? Can a dream change your life?

Throw a Mystery Party!

Who Invited The Stiff to Dinner?
An Interactive Party Game for Teens and Adults
By S. E. Thomas

The guests arrive for a distinguished dinner party at the wealthy English estate of Richard Orwell Mortice. But why would he invite so many of his enemies into his

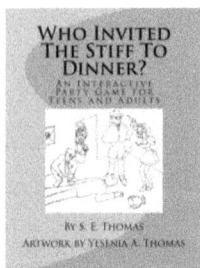

home, along with a Scotland Yard Inspector? When the maid discovers good ol' Rick O. Mortice dead, the Inspector and his overly eager Lieutenant sidekick are out to discover the culprit! Everyone has a motive, and the accusations fly—but not before they go ahead and sit down to a luxurious meal. After all, why let one stiff ruin dinner? *(Requires 15 participants. Includes full, reproducible script, invitation templates, nametags, place settings, and a full set of host/hostess directions. Templates available online for free download.)*

Murder at Surly Gates
An Interactive Party Game for Teens and Adults
By S. E. Thomas

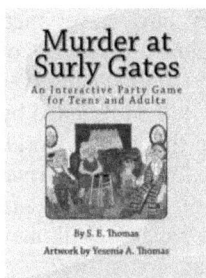

Tensions are high when the cantankerous residents of Surly Gates Nursing Home have to put up with money-hungry relatives, a spoiled brat, and her incompetent mother during visitors' hours. When the nursing home manager turns up dead in his office, everyone is a suspect! Who had something to gain from his death? What happened to Badger's heart pills? Why does Lily, a former beauty queen, still try to swing her hips—even behind her walker? Buster, a resident and former security guard, and his son, Doyle, a bumbling cop, want to solve this case! *(Requires 15 participants. Includes full, reproducible script, invitation templates, nametags, place settings, and a full set of host/hostess directions. Templates available online for free download.)*

Accuracy
An Interactive Party Game for Teens and Adults
By S. E. Thomas

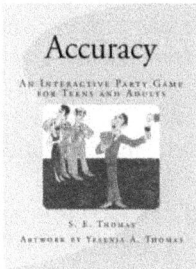

A successful, but pompous, author is murdered on the night of his new book debut celebration. A note—intended to stop the murder—actually spurns the killer into action due to some rearranged punctuation. Who wrote the note? Who tampered with the note? Who carried out the false instructions? Nearly everyone has a motive! An intelligent Spanish lawyer with a very thick accent discovers the truth. *(Requires 11 participants. Includes full, reproducible script, invitation templates, nametags, place settings, and a full set of host/hostess directions. Templates available online for free download.)*

A Full-Length Christmas Production for
Your Church or Christian School!

A Reason To Celebrate
A Full-Length Christmas Production
By S. E. Thomas

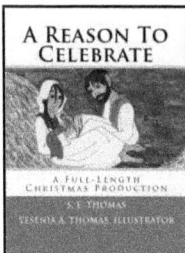

For most, Christmas is a time filled with joy. We gather together with loved ones, feast on delicious food, share mementos of our love for one another, and reminisce about Christmases gone by. But for many, Christmas can be a difficult season. Our fears, the trials that may befall us, and our longings for those we've lost become especially poignant. Some of us may even feel that Christmas is not a time of celebration, but of sorrow.... But let us consider a moment what Scripture tells us of the first Christmas. What really happened? For the first time, God Himself—the Creator of the Universe, the King of Kings, the Everlasting Father—stepped into our world! He stepped in—not to enjoy the wealth or the beauty or the joys—but to experience our suffering, our longings, and our sorrows. And, even from the moment of His birth, He experienced far from ideal circumstances. And yet, we remember His words, "In this world you will have trouble. But take heart! *I* have overcome the world."

Acting Out Loud
Christian Skits and Dramatic Readings
By S. E. Thomas

Whether you are a pastor looking for a skit to help really drive home your message, a ministry leader looking for a dramatic reading to speak God's love at a Christian retreat or conference, or a youth group leader wanting to spice up a youth meeting, we have the material you're looking for! This book offers Biblical skits, skits dealing with issues relating to the Christian walk, evangelistic skits, skits for special events, and holiday skits. Now your audience can experience what it's like to wait their turn in the Hades Complaint Department, learn how to bless others from the Fastest Tongue in The West, or get a glimpse into the hectic life of a pastor through these dramatic presentations that, while fun and entertaining, also deliver a powerful, godly message.

Soon to Come!

A Christmas Romance
An Interactive Party Game for Teens and Adults
By S. E. Thomas

This is a Mad-Lib-Style Party Game! Loads of Fun!
A distinguished widow, Murielle Allan, and her three nearly grown daughters have found that their fortune is

slipping away. The matriarch must marry to insure their future and finds. After years of loneliness, will she choose between a distinguished gentleman or a humble gardener? Meanwhile, she seeks to protect her daughters from the unwanted attentions from men of questionable character. Will she find true love or will destiny destroy her family first? *(Requires 10 participants, a chorus, and a narrator.)*

One Night To Give
An Interactive Party Game for Teens and Adults
By S. E. Thomas

A wealthy but militant woman discovers she is terminally ill and must part with her lucrative boardinghouse. The guests are eager to hear her decision and all have plans for what they will do with the property. Will she give it to her druggy nephew, Homer Stoner, or to her second cousin, Mr. Bill M. Layter? Maybe she'll surprise them all and give it to the highest bidder or to a complete stranger! But what happened to the original owners? Aren't they supposed to be in the Bahamas? An undercover FBI agent is on the case! *(Requires 24 participants.)*

A Nursery Rhyme Christmas
A Full-Length Christmas Production
By Mary Thomas

Little Bo Peep, while looking for her lost sheep, nearly lands on Mother Goose, who is sitting in a manger. Mother Goose also searches for a lamb—Mary's Little Lamb—the Lamb of God who is expected to arrive tonight! Bo Peep wants to find out more about this perfect Lamb. So, Mother Goose elicits the help from Mr. Tortoise, who is slowly but surely beating Mr. Jack Rabbit across the stage, to tell the history of why Jesus was called the Lamb of God and how He would one day save the world from sin. Finally, Mary and Joseph arrive, but there's no room in the Shoe—which is so full of children, the Old Woman doesn't know what to do! Will this precious Little Lamb find a place to rest His head? Who else has heard of His miraculous arrival? Why do the Three Blind Mice Kings speak with Mexican accents? You, your children, and your congregation will LOVE performing or watching this adorable Christmas play, which adapts well-known nursery rhyme characters into a funny and clever—but God-honoring—retelling of the Christmas story!

Please Visit Us Again!

Find books, plays, skits, mystery party games, fundraising resources, writers' services, free downloadable templates, and much more at:

www.thedramaticpen.com

Write To Bless The World

www.ingramcontent.com/pod-product-compliance
Lightning Source LLC
Chambersburg PA
CBHW071927020426
42331CB00010B/2755